# Iceland's Treasured Gifts of Nature

# Iceland's
# Treasured
# Gifts *of Nature*

Iceland
Review

Text © Páll Ásgeir Ásgeirsson 1995
Photography: Páll Stefánsson
English translation: Gary Wake
Printed in Denmark by Nørhaven A/S
Published by Iceland Review, Reykjavik, Iceland, 1995

Front cover: Hraunfossar
Half-title illustration: Reynisdrangar
Frontispiece: From Langanes
Introduction: From Hrafntinnusker

ISBN 9979-51-104-4

# Introduction

At the edge of the Arctic Circle, where darkness retreats from summer's brightness and the sun shines all night long, hidden treasures await discovery by the curious visitors whose path leads there.

At the meeting point of two worlds, the old in the east and the new in the west, and at the edge of the inhabited world, is Iceland.

In the North Atlantic Ridge, which lies north to south like a scar on the bottom of the ocean, a break in the earth's crust constantly moves. In Mother Nature's laboratory eternal creation takes place and thus the volcanic island of Iceland was brought into being. The landscape was cast, waterways formed, mountains filed by glaciers, and thick blankets of lava flooded over everything which came before them. From this comes art, and a land like Iceland has a wealth of valuable gifts that can never be appraised in financial terms – valuables which uplift

the spirit and inspire wonder and awe. Visitors to this land usually leave enriched by the influence of ice and fire.

Iceland is a land of contrasts and diversity where gloriously coloured lava, wide expanses of sand, and the power of its waterfalls all interplay. Mother Nature is mild and warm, or hard and unforgiving depending on the time of year, touching all who encounter her in this land.

The following pages portray some of Iceland's most favoured places which, by their very existence, are proof of the wonder of nature.

# Thingvellir

*Treading on Sacred Ground*

No place is as entwined into the history of this land and nation as Thingvellir. Here, the destiny of the nation and its people was decided in the timeless light of the midnight sun.

At Thingvellir in 930 the Althing was established, one of the world's oldest legislative authorities. It was the parliamentary site for chieftains of the old Icelandic commonwealth until 1262, when Icelanders lost their independence at the hands of the Norwegians. Altogether, the parliament stood here for eight centuries, and it was also here that national independence was proclaimed on the 17th of June 1944. Here, liberty and democracy were born – here is sacred ground.

Not only is Thingvellir the most sacred place in Iceland – it is also special from a geological point of view. At Thingvellir can be seen the effect of the continental drift in the depression between the chasms on either side of the lake, as two opposing tectonic plates shift slowly away from each other.

# Geysir

*King of the Hot Springs*

Old Geysir, king of the world's spouting hot springs, from which they all take their name, now rests in retirement in his crusty hill. Gone are the days of spontaneous eruptions which at their best were often 40-60 metres high.

The hot spring area around Geysir, in Haukadalur valley, is varied and enchanting; one may see different types of hot springs, each with its own personality, though not all capable of erupting. Some are calm and clear, others hiss, spit and boil.

Of the many geysers in the hot spring area, Strokkur, which is shown here, is the liveliest – a kind of prince waiting for his inheritance at the court of King Geysir. Strokkur erupts every few minutes with a splash bringing joy and pleasure to its visitors throughout the year. The boiling water collects in a natural bowl while steam pressure grows in cavities deep beneath until it becomes sufficient for the water to burst upwards and spurt into the air.

# Gullfoss

*The Most Majestic of All Waterfalls*

In a land of a thousand waterfalls it must have been difficult for nature to create one that out-shines all others. With Gullfoss, however, that has been achieved.

Those who bathe their faces in the clear spray from the shining white falls understand that here the cliffs, water and time have created a special work of art.

At Gullfoss, the glittering raindrops in the sunshine at the falls are not just prisms of water, rather sparkles in the eyes of a nation which cherishes its independence above all else.

The waterfall casts itself down two levels totalling 34 metres high through the Hvítá river gorge, which is about 2.5km long and graven from the constant streaming of its waters over the past ten thousand years.

# Hekla

*Entrance to Hell*

In previous centuries it was written in Icelandic travel books that Hekla was the entrance to Hell. The mountain allegedly burned inside and one could hear screams and shrieks of condemned souls carry up through the crater. Overhead, hovering birds with iron claws were ready to snatch those who tried to escape.

Hekla is among the most famous volcanoes in the world and has probably been active for 6,600 years. It has erupted about 20 times since Iceland's settlement. Many of these eruptions have been magnificent but terrifying, lasting months or years and destroying whole areas of the country with tephra and lava. Volcanic clouds sometimes even carried over the ocean.

The mountain grew about 20 metres during the last great eruption in 1947, and stands now at 1,491 metres high. Since then there have been a number of smaller eruptions reminding one that the peaceful exterior masks the hidden strife within.

# Landmannalaugar

*Oasis in the Desert*

Landmannalaugar is a unique geothermal area in the highlands of south Iceland surrounded by desert sands, a blanket of pumice and fields of lava. It is truly like an oasis in a desert. Here it is as if the creator dropped his colour palette while painting the mountains all those centuries ago.

Landmannalaugar lies at 600 metres elevation at the edge of the rhyolite lava which flowed during the eruptions of 1480, creating this highland paradise. Hot pools great for bathing in both the summer and winter, unique ruffled lava, and the gloriously coloured surrounding mountains contribute to the magic of this place.

In the past it was believed that outlaws who stole sheep from farmers lived here, but a search carried out last century failed to find any.

# Torfajökull

*A Well-Kept Secret*

In the mountains south of Landmannalaugar is Torfajökull, one of the smallest glaciers in the country. Torfajökull lies at the heart of an active volcano which last erupted 500 years ago, creating an incredibly beautiful landscape ablaze with all the colours of the rainbow.

The entire area is cut with ravines, ridges and gullies and can be difficult to cross. Many natural treasures, little-known hot springs and colour schemes are concealed in steaming ravines which few have ever seen.

In this place one has to go carefully about, but with a good guide and patience one can get close to the warm heart of the land, which beats fast and with passion for those who approach it with respect.

# Skógafoss
## *White Splendour*

The Skógafoss waterfall tumbles from a cliff right beside the main road at Skógar, under the Eyjafjöll mountain range in south Iceland. It is the last waterfall of the Skógá river, which descends from a height of 1,100 metres with 20 beautiful waterfalls along its course. Skógafoss, though, at 60 metres high, is the most beautiful; it is possible to walk right up to it, coming into close contact with clean, clear water and admire its white splendour and awesome power. It is a singular experience to stand right next to the wall of water and hear its raging noise, feel its cool draught, and sense the earth shiver under foot.

An old story tells of a settler called Thrasi who hid a golden treasure chest in a cave behind the waterfall. Legend has it that one time a beautiful ring was obtained from the side of the chest and kept as a door ring at the church at Skógar.

# Dyrhólaey

## *The Door Stands Open*

**D**yrhólaey is a 120-metre-high sheer cliff head which juts southwards from an otherwise sandy south coast beach west of Vík in Mýrdalur valley. At the end of the tallest spit is an arched tunnel-like doorway through the rock and at low tide it becomes possible to sail a reasonably large boat through it. Daredevils have even flown small planes through the hole for fun.

Dyrhólaey is made of grey granite on its east side and palagonite on its west and has for centuries been a landmark for seafarers approaching the land or traversing the hazardous sea route along the south coast.

A great amount of bird life can be seen on Dyrhólaey and its surroundings, annually attracting large numbers of visitors.

In the sea beyond stand lone pillars of rock and extremely beautiful columnar basalt formations can be found there and on the cliff head.

# Surtsey

*Nature's Laboratory*

Surtsey is the southernmost and youngest of the Westman Islands off Iceland's south coast. It was born during volcanic eruptions between 1963-67 and its birth was a difficult one as the sea was, at the time, 130 metres deep. When the eruptions reached their peak rocks were hurled 2,500 metres into the air and a cloud of ash rose to a height of nine kilometres.

Now Surtsey is quiet as nobody is given permission to visit except scientists, who often travel great distances for the opportunity presented by this rare laboratory of nature. Here, they are able to follow its colonisation by the plants and animals which struggle to survive there. For this reason the island is world-famous and completely unique among its kind.

Furthermore, life here was not slow to take hold as plants, birds and insects soon made this new world their home and habitat.

# Lakagígar

*Remnants of a Cataclysm*

**N**ature has spread a thick carpet of moss over Lakagígar, a long row of craters southwest of Vatnajökull glacier in southeast Iceland. Numbering around a hundred, the craters are both large and small and their variety and glorious colours make this an uncommonly beautiful and peaceful place.

The craters represent nature's warning of mass destruction. They were formed in 1783 during one of the largest volcanic lava eruptions on earth in recorded history. Waterways changed and canyons filled with boiling lava. The consequences were terrible. Farm lands became wastelands and the majority of livestock was killed. A tremendous famine followed in its wake and it is estimated that 10,000 people, almost 20 per cent of the nation, died during the eruption or as a consequence of it. The craters are, therefore, a quiet reminder of the many faces of nature. Stillness and peace can be broken and unstoppable powers unleashed.

# Svartifoss

*Pearl of a National Park*

People have said that in Skaftafell national park the word enchantment has lost its original value. Here, nature speaks in a simple but clear language in setting forth one of the most beautiful landscapes in Iceland.

Skaftafell is adorned with flowers and forested, with clear blue streams and roaring glacial rivers, sharp-edged and dizzying mountains, and the white and rust-brown creeping glaciers. All these are notes in the varied symphony which resounds in Skaftafell year round, and these gentle notes attract many visitors from different places.

The Svartifoss waterfall is one of the most beautiful pearls in Skaftafell. Neither tall nor powerful, its vaults of columnar basalt that surround it make it a memorable masterpiece of nature.

# Öræfajökull

*King of the Mountains*

Öræfajökull glacier towers ice-cold over the fertile lands of Skaftafell national park like a king on his throne. Its peak, Hvannadalshnjúkur, at 2,119 metres, is the highest of the highland mountains. Sharpened peaks stand up from the glacier next to the king, serving to underline his nobility.

Öræfajökull is a part of Vatnajökull, Europe's biggest glacier. It is also, after Mount Etna, the second-largest volcano in Europe and still active. Its eruption in 1362 was one of the greatest pumice eruptions in Iceland, laying whole areas of the countryside to waste, turning it into the desert sands that are seen there today.

Hvannadalshnjúkur was scaled for the first time in 1813 and remains today a popular mountain to climb in both winter and summer. The view can be magnificent, especially when it suits the king to drag off the clouds that often cover him and allow his servants to enjoy the wonders.

# Jökulsárlón

*Unique Lagoon*

Where the glacial river Jökulsá on the Breidamerkursandur sands flows from beneath Vatnajökull glacier, a large lagoon has been created between the glacier edge and the coast. It is of a great depth, about 100 metres, and on it float a vast number of large ice-floes which have broken away from the glacier.

There is nothing like pleasure sailing in between these floating ice enclaves, which provides a unique insight into a cold and silent world broken only by the thudding of ice breaking away from the glacier.

The lagoon is a rather young natural phenomenon because most of it was formed after 1950 when the glacier began to withdraw. Indeed, its existence is already being threatened by the sea which constantly erodes the shoreline.

Nature always holds many secrets and recent studies have revealed that a 20-kilometre-long fjord that nobody has seen leads from the lagoon under the glacier.

# Dyrfjöll

*Residence of the Elves*

T he Dyrfjöll peaks lie towards the north in the East Fjords mountain ridge, and can be seen from a great distance as they reach 1,136 metres to the heavens. The name means mountains with a door, the door being its pass.

At the mountains' roots, in the north, is a tremendous gravel deposit called Stórurd. The landscape there is very colourful, and the nature magnificent. Jóhannes Kjarval, one of Iceland's greatest painters, grew up under these mountains and painted many pictures that feature them.

In this region a belief in elves, trolls, and hidden people flourishes and locals can point out many of their homes in the rocks and stones. It is hardly possible to imagine a more splendid elf palace than right here in Dyrfjöll. It is obvious that creatures from a different world which cherish natural beauty know how to choose a fitting residence for themselves.

# Dettifoss

*Europe's Most Powerful Waterfall*

Visitors to Dettifoss who have found the hairs on the back of their necks rise and felt the rocks tremble beneath their feet from the conflict within this giant of all waterfalls have difficulty believing that this creature could ever be tamed or controlled. The din from the waterfall sits in the consciousness like the song of the country itself and stays with you down all the days. Indeed, Dettifoss has for a long time filled people's souls with inspiration. Many of Iceland's greatest poets have composed poems about it and transformed its power and rage into rhyme and alliteration.

Dettifoss is in the Jökulsá river at Fjöll and is 44 metres high with an average flow of 193 cubic metres per second. It is the most powerful of all waterfalls in Europe and its energy equals 300-400 megawatts. The gorges below the falls are awesome and geologists say they were formed over a short period of time during giant floods of the Jökulsá river.

# Ásbyrgi
## A World of Adventure

sbyrgi is a horseshoe-shaped rocky enclosure with 90-100-metre-high sheer walls on three sides, and a small forest of birch and sallow – a little world of adventure where calm and peace prevail. Within is a beautiful lake where birds rear their young, and their song and the rustle in the birch is the music which nature offers its guests to enjoy.

Ásbyrgi is in Kelduhverfi in north Iceland and according to Norse mythology, it is the hoofprint of Óðin's horse Sleipnir, who had stamped down one of his eight hooves, forming the natural shelter in the process. This happened at a time when people believed in gods who whipped over oceans and lands. Science maintains that it is an ancient river bed that was formed during two gigantic floods of the Jökulsá river 10,000 and 3,000 years ago. What the truth is does not matter because the place is equally beautiful and peaceful either way.

# Mývatn
*Birds, Fish, Flies*

The beauty of Mývatn consists of a limitless variety of colour which can be seen in the lava, water, mountains, flies, trout and birds. The diversity is unbelievable. Each small bay, headland, and every lava bowl is a world in itself where the hard rock and the soft and various vegetation compete for supremacy.

Mývatn is 277 metres above sea level and is named after the midges or black flies that everything in and around the lake live on. It is Iceland's most abundant trout lake during both summer and winter, and it also has unique bird life which attracts enthusiasts from all over the world. More kinds of duck breed here than at any other place on earth and this world of life goes about its daily work screeching, singing and buzzing the whole summer long.

At Mývatn there are pseudo-craters, boiling hot ravines, awesome fissures and lush vegetation that blankets everything. The outcome is a place which is like no other.

# Námafjall

*Where the Land Boils*

Though Iceland seems cold, heat swells beneath. In only a few places does the visible form of heat from the earth appear as ornamental and rich in colour as at Námaskard and Námafjall, just east of Mývatn. Everything here boils and bubbles. The clay swells and simmers in all the earth's many nuances of colours and the land trembles under the feet of tourists in this strange world.

There used to be sulphur mines in Námafjall where sulphur was shovelled together and transported by horse to the coast to be shipped abroad and used in the manufacture of gunpowder. It is the nearest Icelanders have come to producing military munitions for enthusiastic masters of war. However, this industry came to an end during the last century.

Here, boiling pools of mud seem to move according to their own pleasure and free will. They sleep in one place and wake in another with a change of form and new shade of colour, but always with the same strong smell of sulphur.

# Herdubreid

*Rising from the Plain*

erdubreid is an orderly arranged mountain in Mývatnsöræfi, a wilderness near Lake Mývatn. It has received a beautiful and slender form owing to an eruption under a glacier. Herdubreid is 1,682 metres in height and rises steeply 1,100 metres over a broad expanse of lava surrounding it.

It was not until 1908 that the mountain was first climbed, as best is known. Since then many have made their way up but only one way is passable and it is dangerous. However, those who make the journey to the summit receive a rich reward for their troubles, because the view over the glaciers, wasteland and lava is magnificent.

At the foot of the mountain is Herdubreidarlindir, a beautiful lush oasis in the barren wilderness and a popular place to visit. Here it is still possible to see the ruins of Fjalla-Eyvindur's hut; he was the most famous outlaw of the 18th century in Iceland.

# Askja

*Opposites Side by Side*

This old volcanic crater in the eastern highlands reaches 60 metres above the surface of the water within it and has a diameter of 150 metres, but no one knows just how deep the lake is.

The water looks greenish at first, and then milky-coloured the closer one gets. The temperature of the water is comfortable and a more peculiar bathing place would certainly be difficult to find.

The crater's name is Víti, which literally means hell, and it is in Askja. Only a thin verge separates it from Öskjuvatn, which at 217 metres is Iceland's deepest lake, and in contrast with Víti is ice-cold.

This area was formed during a period of terrific volcanic activity in 1875, one of the greatest ash eruptions in Iceland's history.

No one who comes to this place leaves untouched. It is difficult to believe one's own senses while swimming in this green pot which smells of sulphur and clay. Here nature truly blends together and offers up complete opposites.

# Drangey

*The Home of the Outlaw*

The island of Drangey teems with life which in former times was utilised to the fullest. Local men came here to collect birds and eggs in such quantities that the island was called "the milking cow." Today, people still rappel down its cliff faces, though those who come here don't come in hunger, rather to satiate their souls on the awesome beauty and splendour of the life that sings from the edge of every cliff.

Drangey rises about 180 metres above the waves of Skagafjördur fjord on Iceland's north coast and is 0.2 square kilometres in size. The island is composed of palagonite, is sheer, and climbable only in one place. It is the setting for *Grettis saga*, one of the best-known Icelandic sagas. Grettir was an outlaw and strongman who was slain here along with his loyal brother. The story also says that Grettir at one time swam to the shore to attain fire and young men have since followed in his wake, considering it heroic.

# Hvítserkur

*The Petrified Sea Monster*

Hvítserkur is a 15-metre-high rock formation standing at the tide line on three legs, dipping its snout into the sea at the bottom of Húnafjördur on Iceland's north coast.

The name Hvítserkur literally means that which is clothed in a white coat, just as this old monster is. This coat is made of bird droppings, especially from the cormorant which makes for itself a nest on the back and sides of this petrified monster.

Generations have personified this rock and according to national belief old Hvítserkur could be born of livestock kept by trolls. They and their rabble couldn't bear the sunshine on themselves because it would turn them to stone. Undoubtedly this happened to Hvítserkur. His age is reckoned to be a million years and his knees have seemingly begun to buckle under him. Men have needed to strengthen him with cement as the untiring breakers have threatened to topple this giant from his pedestal.

# Drangaskörd

*Sentinels by the Sea*

These magnificent basalt cliffs are known by the name of Drangaskörd and represent one of the most famous outposts in the region of Strandasýsla in the northern part of the West Fjords. They look towards the ice-cold Arctic Ocean and are not exactly on the beaten track because in this area there are no roads, only paths. The highest cliffs are 200-250 metres high while at their outermost and lowest point they are 50 metres high. Silent and unchanging they stand, awakening adoration in the onlooker and a sense of fearful respect.

For centuries people lived here under the harsh conditions their barren land set for them. Driftwood was thought of as a great supplement to farmers, as were fish, birds and eiderdown.

In the past outlaws fled to this distant corner of the land finding sanctuary. It was all witnessed by the cliffs, which could tell many a tale were they to speak.

# Dynjandi

*From Step to Step*

At the innermost point of Arnarfjördur fjord in the West Fjords the Dynjandi waterfall descends in several steps for about 100 metres from a hard cliff edge. The waterfall is 30 metres wide at the top, 60 metres at the bottom and can be seen from afar as a white veil in the awesome landscape of the West Fjords. Its name means noise, or the one making noise.

This waterfall is thought by many to be the most beautiful in the country and it surely is as unique and charming as the fjord itself, whose sharp-edged mountains tower against the sky. In this fjord, beliefs in sorcery and old ways of living survived longer than anywhere else in Iceland.

Now, few inhabitants remain, but the thundering voice of the waterfall still attracts those travelling in this unique part of the country.

# Snæfellsjökull

*To the Centre of the Earth*

Snæfellsjökull glacier sits magically atop a volcano at the very tip of a mountainous peninsula in west Iceland, bathed in the light of the beaming midnight sun. The glacier-crowned volcano is 1,446 metres high and can be seen towering against the horizon, majestic in the clear evening air. It is also one of the most mysterious mountains in the world and many believe it to be one of the earth's true centres. Certainly, the mountain attracts a large number of people, whether in search of supernatural powers, a second youth or just the clean and pure beauty of nature. Most probably find what they are looking for, provided they search hard enough.

The glacier towers over its surroundings as it does in the consciousness of those living in its proximity, who have feasted on its power and live their own lives. As does the glacier.

It is the one and only, and its beauty is eternal.